ANIM
TEAMW

GORILLAS
WORK TOGETHER

ELTON JONES

PowerKiDS press.

New York

Published in 2018 by The Rosen Publishing Group, Inc.
29 East 21st Street, New York, NY 10010

First Edition

Editor: Melissa Raé Shofner
Book Design: Michael J. Flynn

Photo Credits: Cover Danita Delimont/Shutterstock.com; p. 5 Gudkov Andrey/Shutterstock.com; p. 7 (western lowland gorilla) Sergey Uryadnikov/Shutterstock.com; p. 7 (eastern lowland gorilla) Bildagentur Zoonar GmbH/Shutterstock.com; p. 7 (mountain gorilla) FCG/Shutterstock.com; p. 7 (cross river gorilla) https://commons.wikimedia.org/wiki/File:Cross_river_gorilla.jpg; p. 9 Ramon grosso dolarea/Shutterstock.com; p. 11 Thomas Marent/Minden Pictures/Getty Images; p. 13 Andy Rouse/Photodisc/Getty Images; p. 14 Tanya Puntti/Shutterstock.com; p. 15 Dmitry Pichugin/Shutterstock.com; pp. 16–17 Tamas Novak/EyeEm/Getty Images; p. 18 Stephaniellen/Shutterstock.com; p. 19 Edwin Butter/Shutterstock.com; p. 21 Ronald Leunis/EyeEm/Getty Images; p. 22 dean bertoncelj/Shutterstock.com.

Cataloging-in-Publication Data

Names: Jones, Elton.
Title: Gorillas work together / Elton Jones.
Description: New York : PowerKids Press, 2018. | Series: Animal teamwork | Includes index.
Identifiers: ISBN 9781508155522 (pbk.) | ISBN 9781508155461 (library bound) | ISBN 9781508155348 (6 pack)
Subjects: LCSH: Gorilla–Juvenile literature.
Classification: LCC QL737.P94 J66 2018 | DDC 599.884–dc23

Manufactured in the United States of America

CPSIA Compliance Information: Batch #BS17PK: For Further Information contact Rosen Publishing, New York, New York at 1-800-237-9932

CONTENTS

GENTLE GIANTS

Gorillas are sometimes shown in movies and on television as big, angry creatures, pounding their chest and showing their teeth. However, gorillas are actually peaceful animals. They're also very intelligent, or smart.

Gorillas are the largest type of **primate**. They live in close family groups called troops. Each troop has a powerful male leader called a silverback. Gorillas are very social and often use teamwork to take care of their family. The silverback **protects** the troop and leads the members through each day.

CRITTER COOPERATION

Gorillas are apes, not monkeys. Apes don't have tails like monkeys do. Apes also tend to be larger and have bigger brains than monkeys. Apes and monkeys are both types of primates.

The members of a gorilla family are very close. They work together to help each other grow, eat, and stay safe.

TYPES OF GORILLAS

There are two main species, or kinds, of gorillas: western and eastern. Eastern gorillas have two subspecies: eastern lowland and mountain gorillas. Western gorillas also have two subspecies: western lowland and Cross River gorillas.

Mountain gorillas live high in the Virunga Mountains of Africa. They have longer fur than other subspecies to keep them warm in the cold mountains. Eastern lowland gorillas are the largest subspecies. Adult males may grow to be 5.5 feet (1.7 m) tall and weigh up to 440 pounds (200 kg).

CRITTER COOPERATION

Eastern gorillas tend to have blacker fur than western gorillas, which are brownish gray. All gorillas have long arms. They often walk on all fours by curling their hands up and walking on their **knuckles**.

AFRICA

WESTERN LOWLAND GORILLA

EASTERN LOWLAND GORILLA

MOUNTAIN GORILLA

CROSS RIVER GORILLA

Mountain gorillas have a small range and are rare, or uncommon. Cross River gorillas are even rarer. They have a larger range but their population is smaller. They're the most **threatened** gorilla subspecies.

LARGE AND IN CHARGE

Older adult male gorillas are called silverbacks. This is because the fur on their back and upper legs turns silver as they get older. This silver area of fur makes them appear even larger than they are.

There may be up to four adult males in a troop, but only one—usually the oldest and strongest—is considered the leader. The silverback leader is in charge of many things. The leader makes decisions, figures out problems, and provides protection for the troop.

CRITTER COOPERATION

The members of a troop look to their silverback leader to help them find food during the day and places to sleep at night. If a troop has more than one silverback, one may act as a secondary leader.

The silverback leader is usually more than 15 years old. Gorillas may live to be about 35 years old in the wild.

TROOP LIFE

A gorilla troop usually has between five and ten members. Very large troops may have up to 50 gorillas. There are usually several adult females in a troop, along with their young. There may also be several juvenile, or young, male gorillas, which are called blackbacks.

Gorilla troops are **hierarchal** societies, with the **dominant** silverback at the top. The position of adult females depends on when they joined a troop. Those that have been around longer are higher in the hierarchy.

CRITTER COOPERATION

Gorillas stay near their sleeping areas on colder days. If it gets very cold, they may keep each other warm by staying together in a close group.

The silverback leader protects the members of its troop. It's the only male that **mates** with the adult females.

LEADING THE TROOP

Gorilla troops have a plan for their activities each day. They have times for feeding, playing, and even taking a nap! The silverback leader is in charge of what the troop does and when.

Gorillas are most active during the day. At night, larger, older gorillas make beds, called nests, on the ground. Younger, smaller gorillas often build their nests up in trees. Gorillas make new nests each night because they move around to new places in search of food every day.

CRITTER COOPERATION

A troop's members will often begin to grunt—or make short, low noises—at the end of their nap time. This may signal that it's time for everyone to wake up.

Gorillas spend the morning searching for food, then rest during the middle of the day. After they nap, they search for food some more.

13

In the early morning and late afternoon, gorillas search for food. Gorillas mostly eat plant parts such as leaves and roots, though they'll sometimes eat bugs or fruit. However, each subspecies eats different foods based on its **habitat**.

Gorillas wander around and aren't territorial. This means they don't try to keep other animals out of the area of land where they live. Gorillas are peaceful animals with few predators. They may be attacked by leopards and crocodiles, but humans are the biggest threat to them.

CRITTER COOPERATION

Gorillas have great strength and sharp teeth, but they don't often use them to fight. To scare off another animal, they'll first try beating their chest and making loud noises. Silverback leaders of different troops may sometimes fight each other.

Adult gorillas may eat up to 40 pounds (18.1 kg) of food each day. Gorillas get most of the water they need from plants and the dew that collects on them.

STARTING NEW FAMILIES

The silverback leader is the only one allowed to mate with the females in a troop. This means young male gorillas usually leave their family at some point and go off to start their own troop.

When female gorillas are around 8 to 10 years old, they leave their family to find a mate. They often look for a lone silverback to start a new troop with. The first females to join a troop receive better protection from the silverback for themselves and their babies.

CRITTER COOPERATION

Male gorillas often live alone for a few years after leaving their family in order to become stronger and set up their own home range. Most don't start their own troop until they're at least 15 years old.

Adult female gorillas **compete** with each other to be close to the silverback.

BABY GORILLAS

Adult female gorillas usually have one baby at a time, though sometimes they may have twins. Baby gorillas weigh about 3 to 5 pounds (1.4 to 2.3 kg) when they're born. They spend their first six months very close to their mother.

Baby gorillas are very playful. They love to run and roll around with each other. Sometimes they even climb trees. Young male and female gorillas look alike until they're about 8 years old. That's when blackbacks start to look more like older males.

Baby gorillas will ride around on their mother's back until they're two or three years old.

CRITTER COOPERATION

Silverbacks have been seen playing with baby gorillas, too. Sometimes a silverback will even let a baby share its nest.

19

COMMUNICATION IS KEY

Gorillas use their senses of touch, sight, hearing, and smell when **communicating** with each other. Gorillas make many noises to locate each other in their habitat. Scientists believe they make at least 22 different types of sounds to communicate.

Gorillas show how they feel by the way they stand and the faces they make. They don't like being stared at, as this is a sign of **aggression** to them. Silverbacks may give off a strong odor to keep predators away from their troop.

CRITTER COOPERATION

Since the early 1970s, Dr. Penny Patterson has been teaching Koko the gorilla how to use a type of American Sign Language. Today, Koko knows more than 1,000 signs. It's believed she can understand about 2,000 spoken English words.

Scientists believe gorillas feel many emotions, such as sadness, happiness, and love. They're even able to laugh!

CLOSE RELATIVES

Humans and gorillas have a lot in common, including much of their **DNA**. Both have fingernails instead of claws. Gorillas even have fingerprints that are different from one gorilla to the next. Both humans and gorillas also have a range of emotions and use teamwork to take care of their families.

Gorillas are intelligent. They've been known to use branches and other objects as tools. Scientists have also seen young gorillas work together to take apart traps set by poachers, or people who hunt animals illegally.

GLOSSARY

aggression: Forceful or angry actions.

communicate: To share ideas and feelings through sounds and motions.

compete: To try to get something that someone else wants.

DNA: A chemical that contains code that tells an organism's cells what to do.

dominant: The most powerful or strongest; in charge.

habitat: The natural home for plants, animals, and other living things.

hierarchal: Arranged by rank or class.

knuckle: The part of the hand where joints meet and fingers bend.

mate: One of two animals that come together to make babies; to come together to make babies.

primate: Any mammal of the group that includes humans, apes, and monkeys.

protect: To keep safe.

threatened: Likely to be harmed; in danger of dying out.

INDEX

WEBSITES

Due to the changing nature of Internet links, PowerKids Press has developed an online list of websites related to the subject of this book. This site is updated regularly. Please use this link to access the list: www.powerkidslinks.com/atw/gor